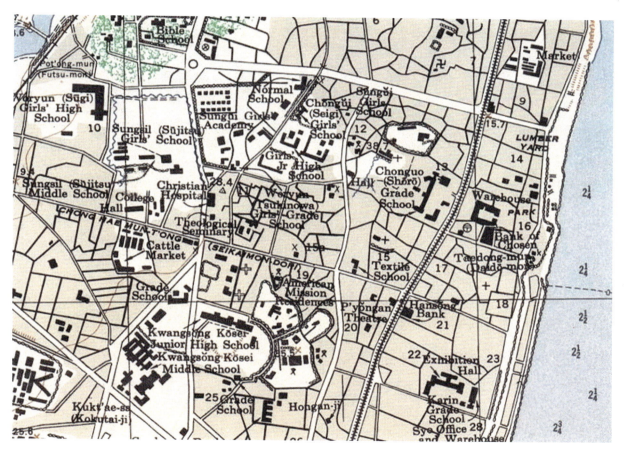

The Presbyterian Mission in Pyongyang, in a Second World War-era U.S. Army map

Front Cover

American mission annual meeting in 1933, in front of Pyongyang Foreign School.

Back Cover

Upper left: West Gate Church in the 1920s

Upper right: Rev. Samuel A. Moffett, founder of the Pyongyang mission

Lower left: Faculty and students of Union Christian College

Lower right: Helen McCune, daughter of George McAfee McCune and granddaughter of Rev. George Shannon McCune, in a Korean dress at three years of age

ISBN 978-1-54-406054-5

(c) Copyright 2017 Robert Kim

Contents

Foreword — 1

The Foundation of the Pyongyang Mission, 1895-1910 — 3

Jerusalem of the East: The Pyongyang Mission, 1911-1936 — 15

Union Christian College — 33

Pyongyang Foreign School — 43

The End, 1936-1942 — 57

The Second World War Generation — 61

American Pyongyang Today — 75

Request for Additional Information / About the Author — 83

Acknowledgments — 84

Notes on Sources — 85

Foreword

The history and photographs presented in this book describe a lost American community in Asia of whose existence few have been aware: the Christian mission of Pyongyang, which from 1895 to 1942 was the center of one of the leading Christian communities on the mainland of Asia. Pyongyang, now known as the capital of North Korea and its militantly atheist government that considers the United States of America to be its mortal enemy, once was a heavily Christian city where American missionaries founded and led the churches, schools, and hospitals. Throughout Korea during the late 19th and early 20th Centuries, American missionaries brought religion, education, science, and the culture and ideas of the West to Koreans eager to embrace them and bring their people and country into the modern world, and the people of Pyongyang and its surrounding region led the entire country in their enthusiasm for the new religion and new outlook on the world. American Presbyterians founded a mission in Pyongyang in 1895, and they and their Korean converts made Pyongyang the most heavily Christian city in Korea and one of the leading centers of Christianity in Asia. The Pyongyang mission's prominence as the headquarters of the Presbyterian Church in Korea and a center of Presbyterian activity throughout Asia led to the missionary community giving the city a dramatic nickname, "Jerusalem of the East."

The Jerusalem of the East ceased to exist during the Second World War, and the Communist regime that took over northern Korea after the war eradicated all remaining traces of it. The escalation of tensions between the United States of America and the Empire of Japan during the late 1930s caused the departure of most Americans from Korea by 1940. After the attack on Pearl Harbor on December 7, 1941, Japanese authorities placed all remaining Americans in Korea under surveillance and then deported them in June 1942, ending an over half century long era of American missionary work in Korea that had begun in 1884. After the end of the war and the liberation of Korea, American missionaries returned to Korea south of the 38th Parallel, but the missions in Pyongyang and north of the 38th Parallel never re-opened, barred from returning by the forces of the Soviet Union occupying the northern half of the country. They and the Communist regime that they installed eradicated the churches and all vestiges of the practice of Christianity in North Korea. Most of North Korea's Christians fled to South Korea from 1945 to

1953, contributing to the society of South Korea becoming one of the most heavily Christian in the world over the course of the 20th Century.

The Americans of Pyongyang have been almost completely forgotten in both Korea and the United States. In South Korea, some memory remains of their role in the growth of Christianity in Korea, but after over 70 years of separation between the north and south, it has become obscure history of a time long ago. In the United States, few were aware of Korea before the Korean War of 1950-53, and when Korea began to enter the national consciousness during and after the war, the American community of Pyongyang had long since disappeared. Its survivors disappeared into the American mainstream, unrecognized by the press, academia, or the general public. This brief photographic history of the Americans of Pyongyang hopefully will help to start the rediscovery of this remarkable American presence in North Korea and its unique contributions to Korea and to the history of the United States of America in Asia.

American Presbyterian Mission Annual Meeting in Pyongyang, 1910s

Chapter 1
The Foundation of the Pyongyang Mission, 1895-1910

The presence of an American Christian community in Pyongyang, inconceivable in the world of the early 21st Century, occurred during a unique period when the people of Korea were emerging from centuries of isolation and Americans were eager to spread their religion and ideas around the world. In the mid-19th Century, Korea was a kingdom that had intentionally isolated itself from outside influences and ideas for over two centuries, leading to the nickname "hermit kingdom" that has stuck since then. After barely surviving an invasion by Japan in 1592-98 that left the country devastated, then repeated invasions by China in the 1630s, the Korean monarchy had imposed a policy of isolation in order to protect the country from further foreign invasions. An aberration in the history of Korea, which had been open to foreign trade and ideas for most of its history, isolation prevented the country from adapting to the Industrial Revolution that had made the great powers of Europe almost unstoppable worldwide and was making Japan the leading power in Asia. By the end of the 1870s, besieged by military assaults and encroachment by foreign imperial powers, the Korean monarchy sought to open and modernize the country in order to defend its sovereignty. Korea established its first modern diplomatic relationship with the United States of America in 1882, and Americans became the leading foreigners advising the king of Korea's efforts to modernize the country's army, economy and education.

Gojong, king/emperor of Korea 1863-1907

American missionaries arrived in Korea soon after 1882. The first was a Presbyterian medical doctor named Horace Allen, who in 1884 obtained permission to proselytize directly from the king of Korea, Gojong. Before then, professing Christianity had been punishable by death, and thousands of Korean converts and foreign missionaries had been executed, as recently as 1866. Dr. Allen arrived in Korea in September 1884 to serve as the physician at the U.S. legation, and after saving the life of a royal family member wounded in a coup attempt in December, he revealed his faith and requested permission to spread Christianity in Korea. The grateful king approved the request, opening the door for Americans and other foreigners to establish churches in Korea. Presbyterian and Methodist missions opened throughout Korea in the years that followed. By 1910, over 400 Americans had served in them.

The Presbyterian and Methodist missions, led by Americans in most of the country with Canadian and Australian Presbyterians in some regions, made rapid progress spreading Christianity in Korea. In 1884, Korea had only small underground groups of Christians converted by French Catholics and Scottish Presbyterians from China. By 1900, there were 60,000 Christians in Korea, 21,000 of them Protestants. In 1910, there were approximately 218,000, 144,000 of them Protestants.

The Presbyterian mission in Pyongyang, founded in 1895, became the center of the most heavily Christian area of Korea. It was the starting point of a wave of conversions in 1907 called the Great Pyongyang Revival, in which thousands embraced Christianity in a movement that spread throughout Korea. By 1910, the Pyongyang area counted over 60,000 Christians in the Presbyterian Church alone. The success of the mission made it the center of the Presbyterian Church in Korea, called "The Jerusalem of the East" in the missionary community.

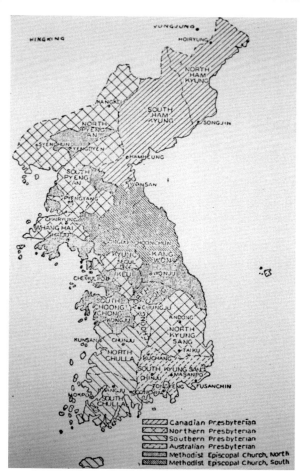

Protestant Mission Territories in Korea

Revs. William Swallen, Graham Lee and Samuel Moffett about to travel from Seoul to Pyongyang in 1895. They traveled by horse because Korea did not have its first operating railroad until 1899, and Revs. Swallen and Lee carried shotguns, likely as protection against guerillas then active in the Korean countryside, some of them violently anti-Christian

The founders of the Presbyterian mission in Pyongyang were Revs. Samuel A. Moffett, Graham Lee and William L. Swallen. Moffett had arrived in Korea in 1890 and visited Pyongyang repeatedly before moving there permanently to found and lead the mission in 1895. Lee joined Moffett in 1895 to serve as pastor of Central Presbyterian Church (founded by Moffett in 1893) and teach at the seminary, which he did until health problems caused him to return to the United States in 1912. Swallen founded and administered schools in Pyongyang and taught at the seminary from 1895 until his retirement in 1932.

The first Presbyterian mission building in Pyongyang, 1895

Second Central Presbyterian Church in Pyongyang

Rev. Graham Lee (left, wearing straw hat) with a visiting missionary, 1897

Presbyterian Council members meeting in Pyongyang, 1901

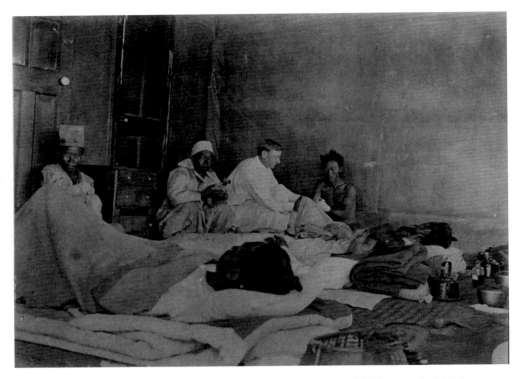

Dr. Wells treating patients at Caroline A. Ladd Hospital, 1906

Saving lives using modern medical science was a central part of the work of the Pyongyang mission to promote Christianity, as it had been for the missions in Korea since Dr. Horace Allen had opened the door for them by saving the life of a relative of King Gojong in 1884.

The foremost medical missionary in Pyongyang was Dr. J. Hunter Wells, who had joined Revs. Moffett, Lee and Swallen in the founding of the mission in 1895 and for 20 years was the leading physician in the city. He saved hundreds of lives during a cholera epidemic in 1895, then became the chief surgeon of the first hospital in Pyongyang, Moffett Hospital, in 1896. In 1906, he became chief surgeon of the new, larger Caroline A. Ladd Hospital, where he served until 1915. He trained and worked with numerous Koreans, including the "cholera corps" that helped him to contain epidemics in Pyongyang.

Dr. Wells with his Korean "cholera corps," "every man many times a hero," August 1902

Dr. Wells' wife Lula became one of several women who founded and led significant programs in the Korea missions. She founded and headed the Lula Wells Institute, a school that provided job training for widows and abandoned wives. It was ahead of its time in assisting destitute women by teaching them skills that they could use to support themselves.

Pyuk Ki Syum Church, in a rural area near Pyongyang   *Rural church congregation*

The Presbyterian mission in Pyongyang spread Christianity also to smaller cities and rural areas throughout northwestern Korea. American missionaries' outreach into rural areas was a central aspect of their approach to their work in Korea, which was unique in following the methods laid down by Dr. John Nevius, a Presbyterian missionary in China who in the 1880s had advocated a new type of independent, self-supporting mission. The Nevius method called for overseas missions to become self-supporting, self-governing entities in which local members would run the churches and support their own church activities, no longer relying on support and leadership from their parent churches in the United States. American missionaries would found missions and train local clergy and laymen to take over leadership as soon as possible. At the same time, they would venture out of their urban missions to spread their message and found new churches throughout the countryside.

The entire region of northwestern Korea around Pyongyang became heavily Christian as a result. For example, the small city of Sonchon, approximately one hundred miles northwest of Pyongyang, became the most heavily Christian city in Korea only a decade after a Presbyterian mission station opened there in 1901. Half of its population of 8,000 had converted to Christianity by 1911.

The rise of Christianity in Korea occurred also because of the connection that emerged between the religion and Korean nationalism. The churches arrived during a time when Korea was besieged by imperial powers and ceased to exist as an independent state. In its first act of imperialism, starting the course that led to war with the United States 65 years later, Japan sent a gunboat to threaten Seoul and imposed an unequal treaty on Korea in 1876. China and Japan engaged in a decade of rivalry in Korea that led to the 1895 Sino-Japanese War, which ended with Japan victorious and dominating Korea's internal affairs. Russia then contended for influence, leading to the 1904-05 Russo-Japanese War that established a Japanese protectorate over Korea. Japan forced King Gojong to abdicate in 1907 and annexed Korea in 1910.

Righteous Army group in a mix of military and civilian outfits

The Korean people attempted to resist but could not stop the rising power of Japan. Popular resistance took multiple forms, among them militias called the Righteous Armies. A tradition almost a thousand years old, since their first uprising in the 10th Century, the Righteous Armies were groups of civilian volunteers who multiple times in the history of Korea rose to fight when the state was incapable of defending the country from foreign invasion. They had been pivotal to defeating the Japanese invasion of 1592-98, but in 1895 they could do little to resist Japan's modern army. Guerilla warfare continued beyond 1910, but it could not stop or even significantly delay the Japanese conquest of Korea.

The churches became new centers of Korean resistance and of movements for national revival. Young patriotic Koreans were among the first to embrace the new religion and the modern, Western ideas that came with it. American-founded churches and schools became places where they became educated, began to organize, and started movements aimed at modernizing the nation and preparing it for independence, in defiance of the Japanese occupation. By the 1910s, Christians were less than 2 percent of the population of Korea but predominated among Korean patriots organizing resistance to Japanese rule.

Girls school of Pyuk Ki Syum Church

Boys school of Moon Pal Church, 1900s

In Pyongyang and throughout Korea, establishing schools was a top priority of the missions. Before the arrival of the churches, education had been only for sons of the aristocracy, educated by private tutors, and illiteracy had been widespread. The churches made education available to the entire people of Korea for the first time by founding schools open to all social classes, and for both boys and girls. Secular schools founded during the same period also had a basis in the American missionary movement. The leader of the first schools founded under the Korean monarchy was Homer Hulbert, an educational missionary who had arrived in Korea in 1886 and whom King Gojong appointed teacher of a school for the royal household and senior aristocrats, then leader and trainer of teachers for the country's first middle schools.

These schools founded by American missionaries became pivotal to the future development of Korea. They popularized the Korean alphabet, *hangul*, which had been created in 1443 but had been rejected in favor of Chinese characters by the country's educated elite. The educated class that the schools created became the source of Korea's leaders during the 20th Century and the first step toward Korea becoming one of the best educated countries in the world.

Dr. J. Hunter Wells (seated, left) and his father Dr. G.M. Wells (seated, right) with four Korean medical doctors, (left to right) Kim Nong Su, Cho Ik Soon, Che Ryong Wha and Kim Pong Chun, the 94th through 97th licensed physicians in Korea, in September 1911

American educational programs included training the first Korean medical doctors. Korean doctors, such as these trained at the medical school of Pyongyang Christian Hospital, took over the duties of many of the medical missionaries.

Union Theological Seminary faculty and students, 1905

The first graduating class of Union Theological Seminary, 1907

The creation of native Korean clergy was another fundamental goal of the missions in Korea, and the first ordination of Koreans as ministers occurred in Pyongyang. Koreans taking over leadership of the churches was intended from the beginning, as part of the Nevius method that called for American clergy to found the churches and then turn over their leadership as soon as possible to local clergy whom they had educated. Rev. Samuel Moffett began the creation of the Korean Presbyterian clergy informally in 1901 by meeting regularly with two students in his home. The Presbyterian Church formally founded Union Theological Seminary in Pyongyang in 1905, the "Union" name reflecting its foundation as a unified multi-national institution by American, Canadian and Australian Presbyterians. The instructors were the founders of the Pyongyang mission in 1895, Revs. Samuel Moffett, Graham Lee and William Swallen, along with William Newton Blair, a Northern Presbyterian missionary who had arrived in Pyongyang in 1901. Union Theological Seminary graduated its first class of seven ministers in 1907.

The elevation of Koreans into the clergy of the Presbyterian Church was a step toward their assumption of leadership roles in the American Presbyterian mission in Pyongyang and ultimately taking over from the Americans who had founded it. Moreover, ordained ministers from Union Theological Seminary would become prominent leaders of Korean nationalist resistance against Japanese rule.

First All Korean Presbytery, 1907

Chapter 2
Jerusalem of the East: The Pyongyang Mission, 1911-1936

1933 American mission annual meeting, photographed in front of Pyongyang Foreign School

From the 1910s to the 1930s, the American mission and the Korean Christian community in Pyongyang continued their leading roles in the growth of Christianity in Korea. Pyongyang (spelled "Pyengyang" before the creation of the McCune-Reischauer system for transliterating Korean in 1937) and the north remained the most heavily Christian part of Korea through to the end of the Second World War in 1945.

The Pyongyang mission and associated mission stations in Sonchon (Syenchun) and other cities, with a Presbyterian missionary community of over 150 Americans for most of this period, grew the church through an array of religious and educational institutions. They fostered the creation of a generation of Christians who became a significant part of the educated class of Korea.

The Pyongyang mission contained numerous institutions for the religious, medical, and educational work of the church. Union Christian Hospital was at the entrance, followed on the same street by West Gate Church and Union Theological Seminary. Numerous schools filled most of the mission compound, along with the residences of American missionary families.

The mission schools began as a private instruction program in 1897 and expanded into a full range of schools for boys and girls from elementary school to college level. Founded by Rev. William M. Baird, a Presbyterian missionary in Korea since 1891, the program became a formal middle and high school in 1900. Sungshil Academy became the name of the school in 1901.

Map of Union Christian College and the Pyongyang Mission, drawn by Evelyn Becker McCune in the early 1930s

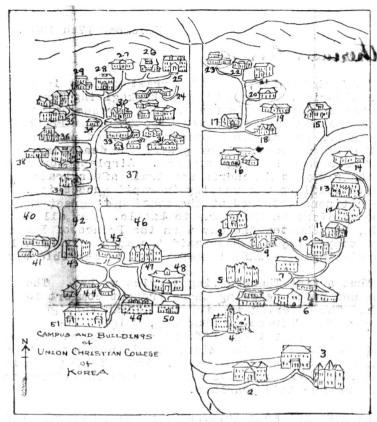

West Gate Church, with Union Theological Seminary visible in the background, 1920s

In 1905, Baird and Arthur Becker, a Methodist educational missionary, founded Union Christian College, the first four year college in Korea.

Pyongyang Foreign School, a private school for the education of the children of mission families and other foreigners in Korea, opened in 1900. Also founded on the initiative of Baird, Pyongyang Foreign School began as a one room schoolhouse with eight children of the mission. It expanded to become a highly regarded boarding school, with over 100 students sent by families throughout Korea and also from China and Japan.

Union Theological Seminary in 1913-14, with the main building on the left and the dormitories on the right

Union Theological Seminary began as a small institution in traditional Korean buildings and soon expanded and modernized. Founded in 1905 with four American instructors and 21 Korean students, and graduating its first class of seven in 1907, within a decade it more than doubled in size. By the 1920s, a modern American-style brick building replaced the original wood building.

The eight American instructors and 25 Korean graduates of Union Theological Seminary in 1916

Union Theological Seminary in the 1920s-30s

Sungshil Academy school for boys building, c. 1910

Sungshil Academy school for girls building, built 1922

The Sungshil Academy and Union Christian College became the leading schools of Pyongyang after their foundation in the early 1900s. The Sungshil Academy educated both boys and girls in separate schools on opposite sides of the mission compound. Union Christian College resided in a large campus occupying most of the southern side of the mission.

One of the students of the Sungshil Academy school for boys in the late 1900s was Kim Hyong Jik, a Presbyterian from a rural area north of Pyongyang who later fathered a son who became Kim Il Sung, the totalitarian leader of North Korea.

Students of the Sungshil Academy school for girls

Union Christian College early campus

Union Christian College in 1928

Pyongyang Red Cross meeting, March 1912. Lula Wells is second from the right in the front row, with several missionary wives, and Dr. G.M. Wells is at the right of the second row.

The mission continued to contribute to the expansion of the medical professions in Pyongyang as well. Dr. Wells and the medical missionaries who followed him trained numerous doctors and nurses at the medical school of the mission's hospital. The growth of the medical professions allowed Koreans to take over the work begun by Dr. Wells in 1895.

Medical school graduation ceremony on July 1, 1914, with Dr. J. Hunter Wells (front row, white suit and hat) the only foreigner present.

By 1915, when Dr. Wells departed Korea, the dependence on expertise from abroad that had prevailed 20 years earlier had ceased. American Christian medical missionaries had succeeded in fostering the emergence of a generation of Korean medical professionals who changed the lives of people in Pyongyang and other cities.

The first three Korean missionaries sent abroad in 1912

First General Assembly meeting in 1912, on the Sungshil Academy athletic field with the boys' school in the background

The Presbyterian Church in Pyongyang also soon progressed beyond the tutelage of the American missionaries who had founded it. In 1912, only five years after the church's first Korean ministers had been ordained, Korean Presbyterians opened a foreign mission of their own, sending three missionaries to China. In the same year, a Korean General Assembly first began regular meetings that assumed increasing leadership over the Presbyterian Church in Korea.

The foundation of an independent Korean Presbyterian Church finally occurred in 1934. It took over leadership of the Presbyterian churches in Korea from the American and other foreign Presbyterian missionaries who had founded and built the church for half a century since 1884. Its headquarters was in Pyongyang, the heart of the Presbyterian Church in Korea since the formation of the Pyongyang mission in 1895.

General Assembly meeting at Mount Kumgang, 1931

General Assembly meeting at West Gate Church, 1934

By the 1930s, Americans in Pyongyang had settled into the role of respected advisers to an independent and self-sustaining Korean Christian community. The men served as clergymen, professors, physicians, and school administrators at Union Christian College, Union Theological Seminary, Union Christian Hospital, and other mission institutions. Women had essential roles in the work of the mission as well. They served as teachers and administrators at the mission's schools for women and girls and also at Pyongyang Foreign School.

Rev. Samuel Moffett and the late Rev. William Blair as "Founders" in the 1932 Union Christian College yearbook

Rev. George and Helen McCune

An outstanding figure among the Americans in Pyongyang from the 1900s to the 1930s was Rev. George Shannon McCune. One of the leading educational missionaries in Korea, he led Presbyterian schools in Pyongyang and its surrounding region, including serving as president of Union Christian College from 1927 to 1936. A supporter of the Korean independence movement and opponent of Japanese imperialism, he was at the center of numerous controversies and repeatedly a target of persecution by the Japanese authorities in Korea for a quarter of a century. For his contributions to education and religion in Korea, the Republic of Korea in 1963 posthumously awarded him its highest honor for contributions to Korean independence, the Order of Merit for National Foundation.

Born and raised near Pittsburgh, George McCune lost his father at the age of twelve and had to work to put himself through school, graduating from Park College in Missouri at the age of twenty-eight in 1901. After working as a college professor and in 1904 marring Helen McAfee, whom he had met at Park College, he became an ordained Presbyterian minister in 1905. George and Helen McCune soon afterward requested to be sent to Korea, which had become the main focus of Presbyterian overseas mission work. They arrived in Pyongyang in September 1905.

George McCune became a central figure in the growth of the schools that the Presbyterian Church was creating in Pyongyang and northern Korea. As superintendent of Presbyterian schools in Pyongyang, he established numerous school throughout northern Korea from 1905 to 1908. He then served as superintendent of Union Christian College in 1908-09 while its founder and president William Baird temporarily returned to the United States on furlough.

George and Helen McCune with their children George (b. 1908), Anna (b. 1906), Shannon (b. 1913), and Helen (b. 1911)

From 1909 to 1921, George McCune served as principal of the Presbyterian school in Sonchon, the most heavily Christian city in Korea, which had become a hotbed of Korean nationalism. In Sonchon, McCune became well known throughout Korea as a supporter of the Korean struggle against Japanese rule. He at first attempted to prevent independence activism at his school, which created the risk of criminal prosecution of his students for sedition, but Japanese persecution compelled him to support the Korean national cause starting in 1911.

In October 1911, McCune became the central figure in mass arrests of Korean independence activists by the Japanese authorities. As part of a campaign that arrested 600 people in Pyongyang and Sonchon, including seven of his teachers and numerous students, he faced false Japanese accusations that he was the leader of a conspiracy by 19 American missionaries and hundreds of Korean Christians to assassinate the Japanese governor-general of Korea.

Korean political prisoners from the One Hundred Five, chained together and blindfolded with wicker baskets over their heads, being marched through Pyongyang

McCune led the defense in the courtroom when 19 American missionaries and 122 Koreans, 98 of them Christians, went on trial as alleged conspirators in June 1912, prosecuted using false confessions obtained by torture. His vigorous defense caused the Japanese court to drop the charges against the 19 Americans and 17 Koreans, but the court still convicted 105 Koreans and sentenced them to prison terms. They included a college president who was vice president of the Korean YMCA, a college professor, and two of McCune's teachers.

Called the Conspiracy Case of 1911 by Americans and the Case of the One Hundred Five by Koreans, the experience was a turning point for McCune. The arrests, torture and imprisonment of his students and colleagues affected him profoundly, and afterward he spoke out against the injustices of Japanese rule both in Korea and while on furlough in the United States in 1913-14. Japanese authorities pressured the Presbyterian mission to remove him in 1915, and mission leaders allowed him to stay only if he avoided possibly inflammatory statements in the future.

March First Movement demonstration

George McCune again became a magnet for controversy during the March First Movement of 1919. The March First Movement, a non-violent revolution in which Korean independence activists read a Declaration of Independence in Seoul and launched nationwide mass demonstrations, directly challenged Japanese rule and required over a month and mass arrests of tens of thousands to suppress. American missionaries were caught completely unaware by the movement and avoided openly supporting it under orders from mission leaders, but Japanese authorities still suspected them of involvement. An instructor at the Sungshil Academy, Rev. Eli M. Mowry, was arrested and sentenced to six months' imprisonment and hard labor after sheltering in his house several of his students fleeing police suppression of a demonstration. McCune faced prolonged official harassment after the demonstrations, which involved the entire student body of his school and practically the entire Christian population of Sonchon.

Japanese police in Sonchon harassed McCune by frequently calling on him and questioning him at length or asking him to come to the police station to explain his movements and his sermons, and in 1921 he began to receive threatening letters, some written in blood, from members of a Japanese ultranationalist organization. Fearing for the lives of their family, and also concerned about the health problems of their elder son George McAfee McCune, George and Helen McCune decided to leave Korea and return to the United States in 1921.

George McCune in 1932

George and Helen McCune returned to Korea in 1927 to serve as president and an instructor at Union Christian College. They returned at the invitation of a new Japanese governor-general in Korea, Kazushige Ugaki, who sought better relations with the Christian missionary community. In addition to heading the leading educational institution in Pyongyang, George McCune served as co-pastor in a church in Pyongyang and a visiting minister in a country district west of the city, and he held numerous leadership positions in the Presbyterian Church and in education. They included serving as president of the Federal Council of Churches in Korea, president of the General Board of Education of the Presbyterian Church in Korea, and organizer and first president of the Educational Association of Korea.

Helen McCune and George McAfee McCune as instructors at Union Christian College

In addition to George and Helen McCune, elder son George McAfee McCune returned to Pyongyang during this period. After graduating from Occidental College in 1930, he taught at Union Christian College in 1931-33. There he became re-acquainted with childhood friend Evelyn Becker, daughter of Union Christian College founder Arthur Becker, and they married in 1933. He returned to the United States for graduate study and earned the first American doctorate in the study of Korea from the University of California at Berkeley in 1941.

1933 ceremony for George McCune's 60th birthday

George McCune's life in Korea came to a sudden end in 1936, when he refused to compromise his religious principles and resisted a Japanese effort to control and assimilate the Korean people. In early 1936, the Japanese provincial governor in Pyongyang demanded that teachers lead their students in visits to Shinto shrines to make offerings to the Emperor of Japan, as a gesture of loyalty. Most teachers and professors complied, but George McCune and other Presbyterians refused, declaring Shinto ceremonies honoring the Emperor, officially considered a god in Japan, to be acts of worship violating the Second Commandment. In retaliation, Japanese authorities stripped McCune of his teaching credentials and placed him under virtual house arrest. Deprived of his purpose and his liberty in Korea, he left in March 1936.

George and Helen McCune resettled in Chicago, where he taught at Moody Bible Institute. He was unable to return to Korea before his passing on December 5, 1941, only two days before the attack on Pearl Harbor that brought the United States into the Second World War.

Rev. George S. McCune (standing before the window), with sons Shannon McCune (second from left) and George M. McCune (far right), granddaughter Helen McCune (in front of George M.), and friends from Korea at a family reunion in Illinois in 1940

Even after the Second World War, the Korean War, and the many other upheavals that occurred after 1936, memory of Rev. George McCune remained strong for several decades in Korea. In 1963, the Republic of Korea posthumously awarded him the Order of Merit for National Foundation, for rendering distinguished service to the cause of Korean independence from 1905 to 1936 through his contributions to education and religion. He is one of the few Americans who have received this honor.

Chapter 3
Union Christian College

Students and faculty in front of the main building of Union Christian College

Founded in 1905, Union Christian College grew into a multi-disciplinary university in a modern American-style campus. The college had programs in the sciences, agriculture, English, music, and other subjects, instructed by a faculty of Americans and Koreans.

Founded by Presbyterians and Methodists and open to Christians of all denominations, Union Christian College drew students from throughout Korea, north and south. It and Chosun Christian College in Seoul were the leading colleges in Korea prior to its division in 1945.

Aerial view of the Union Christian College campus, facing north, showing (left to right) the gymnasium/auditorium, the Sungshil Academy main building, the Library, the Science Hall, the Union Christian College Main Building, and the dormitories.

The Union Christian College campus occupied the southwest quadrant of the Pyongyang mission compound, across the street from Union Theological Seminary and West Gate Church near the entrance to the mission compound. After two decades of building from 1905 to the 1920s, the campus had modern buildings identical to those on American college campuses that housed the college's academic programs and students. The largest building was the combined gymnasium and auditorium in the southwest corner of the campus, used for basketball and other sports and for large meetings and ceremonies.

All of the photographs in this chapter show the campus and its buildings in 1933, when they were complete and identical to their state in 1945.

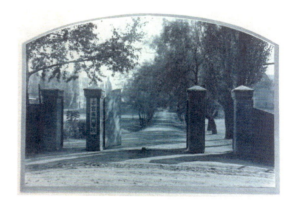

Entrance to the campus

The Main Building

Science Hall

Sungshil Academy, Library and Founder's Memorial Stone

Gymnasium/Auditorium and Agriculture Laboratory

New Dormitory

Basketball tournament on a court outside of the Sungshil Academy boys' school

Union Christian College gospel team, which traveled around the country to evangelize, summer 1921

Class excursion to Peony Hill (Moranbong), now the location of major North Korean structures such as Kim Il Sung Stadium and the Victory Arch

Graduation ceremony on the Union Christian College athletic field, with straw boater hats worn by most men and American football goalposts visible on the right

Teams in the three most popular sports: soccer, basketball, and tennis

Sendoff ceremony for the Union Christian College football team, about to depart to Seoul to play archrival Chosun Christian College

Chapter 4
Pyongyang Foreign School

Teachers and Students of Pyongyang Foreign School, 1934

Founded in 1900, Pyongyang Foreign School grew from a one room schoolhouse with eight children to a boarding school with over 100 students by the late 1920s. In addition to children of the Pyongyang mission, the students were from throughout Korea and also from families in Japan and China. Families of American missionaries and businessmen throughout Asia sent their children to the school, which had a reputation as the leading school for Americans in Asia.

The entire school in 1904 - two teachers and nine students

The school in 1906

The school in 1912

1932 school photo

1933 graduating class

Pyongyang Foreign School was located on the west side of the mission compound, just north of Union Christian College. From 1900 to 1940, it occupied several different buildings: a first schoolhouse in 1900, an immediate replacement used in 1900-08, a larger schoolhouse in 1908-25, and the final building that it occupied from 1925 to 1940. Dormitories for boys and girls occupied the area just north of the schoolhouse along the western edge of the mission compound.

First schoolhouse, 1900

Boys' and girls' dormitories

Pyongyang Foreign School, 1925-40

From 1900 to 1940, a total of 584 students attended the school, of whom 188 graduated from the high school. Reflecting the unusual demographics of the mission, in which almost all of the American population consisted of clergymen, medical doctors, professors, and their families, practically all of the school's alumni went on to attend college at a time when fewer than five percent of Americans had college degrees, and approximately 30 percent joined the ministry or other religious work or entered the medical professions as medical doctors or registered nurses.

The school replicated much of the activities and lifestyle of a private school of its era in the United States. In addition to academics, boys and girls competed in a variety of sports. Basketball and tennis were popular for both boys and girls. Boys had an ice hockey team in the winter and a soccer team in the spring. Girls also had volleyball and field hockey teams. These teams competed against Korean schools in Pyongyang, Union Christian College, and Chosun Christian College in Seoul.

Girls' athletics, from the 1933 Pyongyang Foreign School yearbook. In the field hockey team photo, sixth from the left is Ruth Bell, a daughter of Presbyterian medical missionaries in China, later Ruth Graham, wife of Rev. Billy Graham.

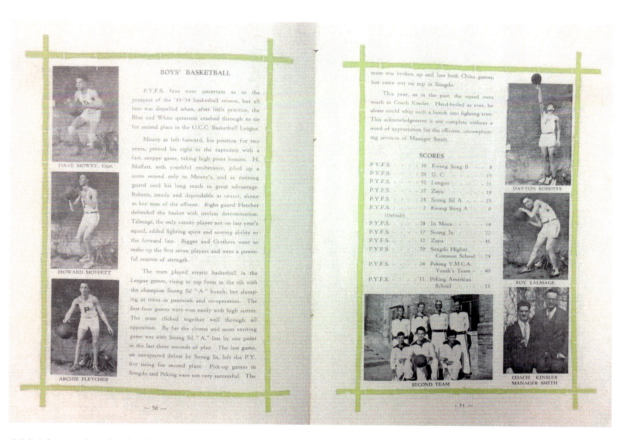

1934 boys' basketball team history, which included a foreign trip for games in Peking, China.

Pyongyang Foreign School hockey team, 1934. This team included goaltender Samuel H. Moffett and defenseman Howard Moffett, sons of Pyongyang mission founder Rev. Samuel A. Moffett, and left wing David Mowry, son of Rev. Eli Mowry, who had been imprisoned after the March First Movement of 1919.

Pyongyang Foreign School and Chosun Christian College hockey teams meeting on the frozen Taedong River in 1933

The Pyongyang Foreign School ice hockey team played regularly against the best team in Korea. Most of its games occurred in Pyongyang against a neighboring Korean high school, Kwangsung School, with occasional games against its main rival American school, Seoul Foreign School. The big game each year was against Chosun Christian College, the top hockey team in Korea, which had won the first Korean national championship in 1930 and regularly won national championships during the 1930s. (Chosun Christian College's dominance of Korean hockey continued after the Second World War and into the 21st Century, under the college's new name, Yonsei University.) Chosun Christian College's team traveled to Pyongyang each year to play against Pyongyang Foreign School. Games occurred on Pyongyang Foreign School's outdoor ice rink or on the frozen Taedong River, which in northern Korea's harsh winters often froze solid.

1936 game against Chosun Christian College on the Pyongyang Foreign School rink

Action in front of the Pyongyang Foreign School goal in the 1936 game with Chosun Christian College

Pyongyang Foreign School regularly beat Kwangsung and Seoul Foreign School by lopsided margins but could not compete successfully against the greater maturity, size and skill of Chosun Christian College. Against Chosun Christian College, Pyongyang Foreign School lost 5-2 in 1933, and in the following year they played a hard-fought game to a scoreless tie, with play hampered by heavy snow during the third period. Chosun Christian College continued to elevate its game for the rest of the decade, however, becoming practically impossible for a high school team to compete against. In 1936, the record states only that an overmatched Pyongyang Foreign School "lost by a wide margin" to Chosun Christian College, having "succumbed to the superior weight and experience of the college men."

Boy Scout Troop 1 of Pyongyang, 1932

Boy Scout Troop 1 of Pyongyang was open to boys of Pyongyang Foreign School. As a branch of the Boy Scouts of America, the troop was one of the few organizations to fly the American flag in Pyongyang under Japanese rule.

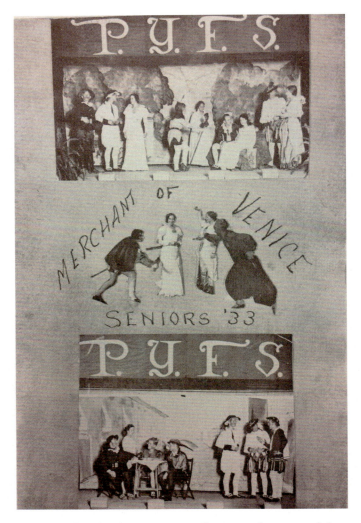

Poster for the 1933 senior class production of the
Merchant of Venice

For students interested in the performing arts, there were the school band and glee club, and an annual Shakespeare stage production.

SOCIALS

HALLOWE'EN FETE

The High School was unrecognizable in the garb of book characters. Over the leaf-covered floor of the Gym drifted Humpty-Dumpty, Bluebeard, Heidi and Peter, Priscilla, Helen of Troy, Polly Flinders, Aladdin, Boy Blue, Robin Hood, Hans Brinker, Sir Boss, Lawrence of Arabia, Mme. Lafarge, Ophelia, Peter Pan and Wendy, and best of all the Horse of Troy (see picture) which loped and floundered through the assemblage led by Aeneas resplendent in an aluminum-kettle-helmet.

Refreshments were served in clever fashion and after fifteen rahs (see unwritten Constitution of P. Y. F. S.) for the Juniors and Freshmen who gave the party, everyone scampered off to the last basketball game of the League which our team won.

1933 Halloween party story

THE VALENTINE PARTY

All aboard! We're off for the moon. Groups of boys and girls collected in the two rooms fixed as the lounge and the sun room of a rocket ship. While the 1st Officer was giving out riddles in the lounge the other group joined hands in a circle about a row of ten pins. Each person tried to swing one of his neighbors against a ten pin. Those who bumped against them and knocked them down were out. An exchange of rooms was then made and also an exchange of partners. While some were endeavoring to hit with erasers full moons hung on strings, the others made up telegrams from specially assigned letters. Many puzzled couples figured over such letters as x-y-w-p-p-m-z-x. Suddenly they reached the moon with a terrible jolt. Everyone left the rocket on the second story and descended to the moon. The auditorium was transformed into a weird blue world. Colored streamers hung all about. A volcano was seen at one end of the room and swirling streamers and music issued from it. Suddenly out from a volcano at the front of the moon stepped the Lady of the Moon dressed in red and silver. Here under the spell of the moon the boys were made to propose to three girls, each receiving a score for his efforts. The three having the highest total were made to propose to the Lady of the Moon and the winner claimed her for a partner for the trip back to the earth.

Back again in the rocket the Sophomore girls served punch, sandwiches, and peanuts to everyone. After a short trip the rocket landed with a terrible roar and screaming of the engines and the strange trip was ended.

THE SCOUT PARTY

"Uh—er—Has, um, anyone asked you to the Scout Party?" "No." "Well, may I—er—take you?" "Why—yes."—And therefore, on the 22nd of February, certain young gentlemen took certain young ladies to a party at the Gym. As each girl entered the door she drew a ticket which assigned her and her escort to one of four groups—namely, the Cuckoos, Hyenas, Jackals, or Rams. Everybody howled and baa-ed and cuckoo-ed as hard as he could for a while, until Mr. Chandler directed some contests of various sorts. Table soccer supplied frequent gusts, and other merry games wore the evening away, till the Jackals served cake and ice cream while Mr. Shaw led the "smile song." After refreshments everybody gathered into a circle and sang. Then Taps was sounded and the evening was over.

More party stories from the 1933 yearbook

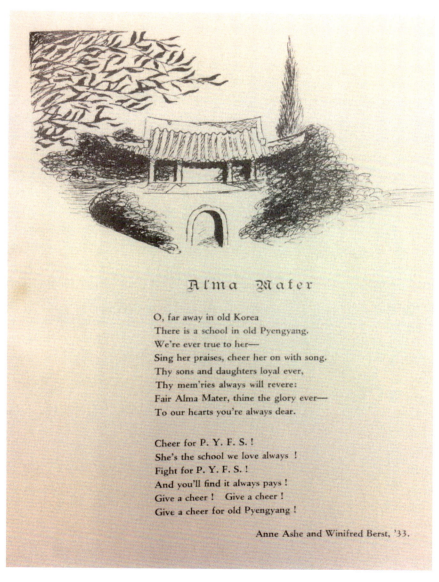

Pyongyang Foreign School song

Chapter 5
The End, 1936-1942

1938 American mission annual meeting at Pyongyang Foreign School

The American Christian presence in Pyongyang began to recede in 1936 as Japan sought to assert greater control over the Korean people in its empire, and after the attack on Pearl Harbor and the start of war between Japan and the United States, it ceased to exist after 47 years of central importance in Pyongyang.

The imposition of Shinto worship of the Emperor of Japan on Christian schools and the expulsion of the Rev. George S. McCune in 1936 were the beginning of the end, starting the withdrawal of Americans from Pyongyang and Korea from 1936 to 1942. In 1938, a wave of departures of Presbyterian missionaries from Pyongyang and Korea began. After Rev. George McCune's refusal to conduct Shinto ceremonies at Union Christian College, the Presbyterian Church agreed with his stance that obeying the Japanese order would violate the Second Commandment, and as a result in 1938 the Presbyterian Church closed its schools in Korea, including Union Christian College in Pyongyang, and withdrew its educational missionaries. The Pyongyang mission continued, significantly reduced, with the churches, hospitals and Pyongyang Foreign School remaining open. In the fall semester of 1940, there were still 105 students enrolled at Pyongyang Foreign School, 55 of them from families living in China, Manchuria and Japan.

Pyongyang Foreign School, 1940

The last mission meeting in Pyongyang, on March 3, 1941

In 1940 another wave of departures occurred that almost completely closed the American Christian missions in Korea. With war between Japan and the United States seen as imminent, in October 1940 the U.S. Department of State issued a warning that all American citizens should leave Asia and return to the United States. The mission boards reacted by recalling most of their people, and approximately 400 Americans hastily left Korea. They included the entire student body and faculty of Pyongyang Foreign School, who shut down the school and evacuated in only five days after receiving the school board's decision to close the school.

By July 20, 1941, only 126 Americans remained in all of Korea, 109 of them missionaries and their family members. More departed in November 1941 as the mission boards recalled more of their missionaries.

*The MS Gripsholm arriving in New York with Americans
interned in Korea, Japan and elsewhere in Asia*

After the Japanese attack on Pearl Harbor on December 7, 1941, the Japanese authorities placed the remaining Americans in Korea under police surveillance and in April 1942 forced them to leave Korea in an exchange for Japanese civilians in the United States. The last 99 Americans in Korea, 21 of them Presbyterian missionaries, were sent to Maputo in Portuguese East Africa (now Mozambique) on a Japanese ship, then transferred to the neutral Swedish passenger liner MS *Gripsholm* for a voyage to New York and repatriation to the United States.

American Pyongyang had disappeared, 47 years after its foundation, its people scattered around the United States in a country mobilizing for a world war against Japan, Germany and the Axis powers.

Chapter 6
The Second World War Generation

With a generation of Americans having been born and raised in Pyongyang from the 1900s to the 1930s, many children of American Pyongyang served in the U.S. armed services or as civilians involved in the war effort during the Second World War. The following are a few examples of the men and women from Pyongyang who served in the war and a list of those who served after attending Pyongyang Foreign School.

George McAfee McCune

George and Evelyn McCune with their daughters Helen (left) and Heather (right) and his cousin Mildred McAfee (left), president of Wellesley College from 1936 to 1949 and director of the U.S. Navy WAVES (Women Accepted for Volunteer Emergency Service) from 1942 to 1945.

George M. McCune, elder son of the Rev. George S. McCune, became a pioneering American scholar of Korea and the U.S. government's main Korea expert during the war. He created the McCune-Reischauer system for transliterating Korean and in 1941 earned the first doctorate in the study of Korea in the United States. Immediately after the attack on Pearl Harbor, the new intelligence service that became the Office of Strategic Services (OSS) hired him as its expert on Korea. His 1942 intelligence report on Korea became the basis for OSS planning throughout the war. In 1944, he became the Korea desk officer for the Department of State's Far Eastern

Division. From then to the end of the war, he struggled to inform U.S. political leaders about Korea and advocate for U.S. efforts to preserve the independence and unity of Korea.

After the war, George McCune became a professor teaching Korean studies at the University of California at Berkeley. Afflicted with heart problems since childhood, which were worsened by working to exhaustion during the war, he died at the age of 39 in November 1947, shortly after the division of Korea.

Evelyn Becker McCune

Evelyn Becker McCune, daughter of Union Christian College founder Arthur Becker and wife of George M. McCune, was a Korea scholar in her own right who served as a civilian in both the Second World War and the Korean War.

During the Second World War, she served as a civilian expert on Asia for several U.S. government agencies. She served as a volunteer assistant in the Far Eastern Section of the Committee on the Protection of Cultural Treasures in War Areas, an organization that supported the "Monuments Men" overseas by preparing lists and maps of cultural monuments overseas. She also worked for the Army Map Service, making U.S. military maps of Korea.

From 1945 to 1950, she earned a master's degree and continued George's work at UC Berkeley, including completing and publishing his posthumous book *Korea Today*, which became a bestseller when its publication in 1950 coincided with the outbreak of the Korean War.

Evelyn Becker McCune after the war with daughters Helen and Heather

During the Korean War, she worked first as a Korea expert for General Douglas MacArthur, who sent her to Seoul immediately after the landing at Inchon to find and recover artifacts looted by the North Koreans from the National Museum of Korea. In 1951-52, she founded and headed the Korea unit at the Library of Congress, educating members of Congress on the little-known country where the United States was at war. In 1952 she went to Korea and Japan for the State Department and the Library of Congress, and in 1953-54 she served as a liaison officer for the United Nations Reconstruction Agency. In 1962-63 she again worked for the State Department, conducting research on North Korea for the Bureau of Intelligence and Research.

Evelyn McCune taught in Korea and Japan for the University of California Overseas Program in 1954-55 and at Diablo Valley College in 1956-78, and she authored numerous books and articles on Korean art and culture. In 1982 she received an honorary doctorate from Yonsei University, where her father had been one of the founders in 1915. She passed away in California in 2012 at the age of 105.

Maxwell Becker

Maxwell Becker (back row, left) at age 17 with the Seoul Foreign School basketball team

Maxwell Becker, son of Arthur Becker and brother of Evelyn Becker McCune, was a star athlete at Pyongyang Foreign School, Seoul Foreign School, and UC Berkeley who became a U.S. Forest Ranger during the 1930s and a lieutenant colonel in the U.S. Army during the Second World War.

Becker became an expert on escape and evasion tactics for MIS-X, a top secret organization responsible for the rescue of downed U.S. airmen, and in August 1943 he deployed to China as a deputy commander of the Air Ground Aid Section (AGAS), a special operations force that rescued thousands of Allied airmen, prisoners of war and civilians in China and Southeast Asia. He conducted rescue missions from the Himalayas to the coast of China, often parachuting deep behind enemy lines to locate and rescue lost airmen and POWs.

The latter included five survivors of the Bataan Death March who in October 1944 barely survived the sinking of their POW transport ship, the *Arisan Maru*, which took the lives of 1,773 Allied POWs and civilians. Becker parachuted hundreds of miles behind Japanese lines to find the five survivors on the coast of China and escort them to safety with General Claire Chennault's Fourteenth Air Force in Kunming.

After the war Becker returned to forestry, advising forestry programs overseas in Korea, Bangladesh, Chile and Honduras. In his retirement he returned to the religious and educational missionary work of his father, founding churches and The Becker School in Honduras. He passed away in 2001 at the age of 92.

Captain Maxwell Becker with daughters Maxine and Marilyn before deploying to China in 1943

Shannon McCune

Shannon Boyd-Bailey McCune, the younger son of Rev. George S. McCune, had a distinguished academic and government career from 1939 to 1979 that included wartime service in India and China. Born in Sonchon in 1913, he received the Korean name Yun An-Paik, the "Peaceful Hundredth," at the request of the 99 Koreans imprisoned in the Case of the One Hundred Five, as a symbol of solidarity between them and the McCune family. He began teaching geography at Ohio State University in 1939 and in early 1942 became Chief of the Korea-Manchuria-Formosa Unit of the Enemy Capabilities Branch in the Office of Economic Warfare (OEW). In 1944-45 he served in India, Ceylon and China with the Foreign Economic Administration. He was awarded the Presidential Medal of Freedom for his work in China in 1946. After the war he was a professor or administrator at several universities including Colgate University, the University of Massachusetts and the University of Florida, and he served as the first civil administrator of Japan's Ryukyu Islands in 1962-64. He passed away in 1993 at the age of 79.

Shannon McCune (right) and friend Horace Sharrocks (left) with Rev. Paik Yang Chun, a friend of Rev. McCune who had baptized them

Shannon McCune in 1965

Pyongyang Foreign School at War

The following is a list of students of Pyongyang Foreign School who during the Second World War era served in the U.S. armed forces, worked as civilians for the U.S. government or in American war industry, or served in other Allied armed forces or governments, including those of the United Kingdom, Canada, and Australia. It lists 85 of the approximately 600 individuals who attended Pyongyang Foreign School from its foundation in 1900 to its closing in 1940. By 1943, two were known to have been lost, 2nd Lt. Archibald Campbell Jr., Army Air Corps, killed in a crash landing in May 1941, and Dwight Emerson Thompson, missing and presumed dead as a civilian working for the Office of Lend-Lease Administration in Burma in April 1942.

The number of Pyongyang Foreign School students who served in the Second World War was comparable to the 12 percent of the U.S. population that served in the U.S. armed services during the war, and the number would have been higher if not for the unusual demographics of the school. Approximately 30 percent of the graduates of Pyongyang Foreign School entered the clergy or the medical professions, and many of them volunteered for military service, but others had responsibilities that kept them in the United States as civilians.

This information is from a comprehensive list of former Pyongyang Foreign School students compiled for a master yearbook reporting the entire history of the school, *The Master Kulsi*, published in 1943. It was acknowledged to be incomplete because of the difficulty of finding and obtaining responses from widely scattered individuals under wartime conditions, but it provides an indication of the ways in which Americans born and raised in Pyongyang served their country during the Second World War.

	Pyongyang Foreign School years (* graduated)	Military or Civilian Service
Rea Hurvey Allison	1934-38	U.S. Marine Corps
Paul Parker Anspach, II	1935-39 *	Intelligence, U.S. Navy

Name	Years	Service
Sylvia Carolyn Anspach	1934-38 *	Occupational analyst, Air Service Command, U.S. Army
Evelyn Becker (McCune)	1913-14	Far Eastern Section of the Committee on the Protection of Cultural Treasures in War Areas, and Army Map Service
Charles Kirkwood Bernheisel	1914-25	U.S. Army
Helen Francis Bernheisel	1919-33	Army Ordnance Plant, Indianapolis, Indiana
John Dinsmore Bigger, Jr.	1920-31	Ordnance Department, Washington, DC
William Parker Bigger	1921-34 *	Weather observer, U.S. Army Air Corps
Edgar Allen Blair	1918-30 *	U.S Marine Corps
Wilmot Burgess Boone	1927-28	1st Lt., U.S. Army Medical Corps
John Mead Boots	1932-34	Lt. (jg), U.S. Navy, USS Hughes (DD-410)
Edwin Everett Braden	1929-35 *	Specialist 2nd Class, U.S. Navy
Arthur Leslie Bridgman	1937-39 *	U.S. Army
Harold Thomas Bridgman, Jr.	1937-40	Cadet, U.S. Army Air Corps
George Thompson Brown	1937-38 *	1st Lt., U.S. Army
Edmund Burgoyne	1924-31	Secretary, British Consulate, Chungking, China
Eileen Burgoyne	1924-27	Private Secretary, Shanghai, China

Archibald Campbell, Jr.	1930-34	2nd Lt., U.S. Army Air Corps, killed in forced landing May 1941
Helen Van Ess Clapham	1929-38 *	U.S. Navy WAVES
William Arthur Clapham	1925-33 *	Lt., U.S. Navy Air Service
Charlotte Marie Cline	1931-35	U.S. Navy WAVES
Theodore Noel Cline	1933-35	Aviation Cadet, U.S. Navy
Samuel Dunlap Crothers	1925-35 *	Chaplain, Lt., U.S. Navy
Edward Henry Currie	1938-40 *	U.S. Army Air Corps
Vester John Dick	1934	Corporal, U.S. Army Engineers
Stephen Inslee Dodd	1929-33 *	1st Lt., U.S. Army Medical Corps
George Livingston Erdman	1920-21, 1923-24	1st Lt., U.S. Army Medical Corps
John Duncan Fraser, Jr.	1932-35	U.S. Navy
John Stiles Fraser	1931-37	1st Lt., Canadian Army
Charles William Harrison	1924-28	Major, U.S. Marine Corps
Richard Pusey Henderson	1932-39 *	1st Lt., Canadian Army
Robert Stephen Hill	1929-40	U.S. Army
Donald Vincent Hirst	1930-33 *	1st Lt., U.S. Army Medical Corps
William Thomas Hopkins	1939-40	Private, U.S. Army
Donald Campbell Kerr	1929-30	Ensign, U.S. Navy Reserve
James Wilson Kerr, III	1933-38 *	1st Lt., Infantry, U.S. Army

Elmer Gordon Kiehn	1936-38 *	U.S. Navy, Assistant Communications Officer, USS Breckinridge (DD-148)
Helen Cordelia Lampe	1926-33 *	1st Lt., Nurse, U.S. Army
Henry Willard Lampe	1926-30 *	1st Lt., Chaplain, U.S. Army
James Sharrocks Lampe	1935-40	Cadet, U.S. Navy Aviation
Nathan Chambers Lampe	1928-33	Staff Sergeant, U.S. Army
Elmer Athalone Levie	1935-40	Army Air Corps
James Kellum Levie, Jr.	1928-34	1st Lt., U.S. Army, captured on Bataan Feb. 1942
Frank Walter Lilley, III	1934-36	Officer Candidate, U.S. Army
Hugh MacIntyre Linton	1939-40	U.S. Navy
William Alderman Linton, Jr.	1936-40 *	U.S. Army, Japanese Language School
Shannon Boyd-Bailey McCune	1928-31 *	Office of Economic Warfare and Foreign Economic Administration
Harriet Elizabeth Moore	1924-37 *	Librarian, Navy Base Library, Norfolk, Virginia
Maie Phila Newland	1936-40	Secretary, U.S. Army Air Corps
Thomas Wills Newland	1928-33 *	Ensign, U.S. Navy
Harold Joyce Noble	1910-12	Captain, U.S. Marine Corps, 3rd Marine Division
William Lawrence Parker	1928-35	U.S. Army Air Corps
Charles Lunch Phillips, Jr.	1924-35 *	1st Lt., Aviation Instructor, U.S. Army Air Corps

James Potter Phillips	1927-38	2nd Lt., Aviation Instructor, U.S. Army Air Corps
John Fairman Preston, Jr.	1923-25	Medical Superintendent, Volunteer Ordnance Works, Chattanooga, Tennessee
Rhea Sutphen Preston	1936-40 *	Medical Corps Replacement Center, Fort McClellan, Alabama
William Wiley Preston	1928-32	U.S. Army, 668th Engineer Topographic Company
Robert Wesley Randall	1939-40	Private, U.S. Army
David Abernethy Reeder	1933-36	U.S. Navy Reserve Naval Language Unit, Boulder, Colorado
Donald Eugene Reiner	1919-30	Major, U.S. Army Medical Corps, Base Surgeon, McChord Field, Washington
Philip Charles Reiner	1929-40	Dental Student, U.S. Army
Ralph Everett Reiner	1919-30	Major, U.S. Army Medical Corps, 55th Operational Training Wing, MacDill Field, Florida
David Ross Rogers	1933-38 *	Medical Student, U.S. Navy
Joseph Alexander Romig	1928-31 *	Ensign, U.S. Navy, USS YMS-288
Robert Davis Ross	1934-37	Royal Canadian Air Force, Spitfire pilot
Elmer Boyd Scott	1938-39	Royal Canadian Air Force, pilot
Kenneth Munro Scott	1927-31	U.S. Army Medical Corps
William Hamilton Shaw	1928-39 *	U.S. Navy Reserve officer training
Kenneth McLane Smith	1924-30 *	Captain, U.S. Army Medical Corps

Name	Years	Service
Robert Bigger Smith	1926-31 *	1st Lt., U.S. Marine Corps
Willis Snyder	1929-30	U.S. Navy
Mary Swallen		Registered Nurse, U.S. Army
Hampton Venable Talbot	1933-37 *	U.S. Army
Roy Van Neste Talmage	1927-34 *	U.S. Army Air Corps, Maxwell Field, Alabama
Dwight Emerson Thompson	1929-33 *	Lend-Lease program civilian employee in Burma, missing and presumed dead about April 19, 1942
Reuben Archer Torrey, III	1932-34 *	Merchant Seaman
Edmund Lorenz Van Deusen	1936-37	Corporal, U.S. Army
John Watson	1921-22	Australian Army Medical Corps
Benjamin Burch Weems	1929-31 *	Intelligence Analyst, War Department
Victor John Wiens	1935-39 *	Private, U.S. Army
James Stephenson Wilson	1925-29	Captain, U.S. Army Medical Corps
Mary Stuart Wilson	1926-32 *	Lab Technician, Hercules Powder Plant, Richmond, Virginia
Thomas Edwin Wilson	1933-36	2nd Lt., U.S. Army
Allan Rodgers Winn	1923-25	Chaplain, U.S. Navy Reserve, Brooklyn Navy Yard
Ruth Eileen Winn	1923-25	Red Cross Military Welfare Service Overseas Unit

Douglas Hills Wright, Jr.   1934-35   Officer Candidate School, U.S. Army

Pyongyang Foreign School Members Imprisoned By Japan

Some Americans from Pyongyang were living overseas in areas of Asia that Japan conquered and occupied in 1941-42. Instead of being exchanged for Japanese civilians and repatriated to the United States soon after the start of hostilities, like Americans who had remained in Korea, they experienced prolonged internment in Japanese prison camps. They included the following individuals who had been students at Pyongyang Foreign School in the 1920s and 1930s and were captured in the Philippines and China in 1942.

	Pyongyang Foreign School years (* graduated)	Country Where Interned
Mary Luce Boone (Vinson)	1927-28	Philippines
Paul Frederick Donnelson	1936-37	China (Shanghai)
William Brewster Mather	1927-28	Philippines
Lilian Ross	1930-35 *	Philippines
Gardner Lewis Winn	1923-25	Philippines
Paul Rutherford Winn	1928-30 *	China (Shanghai)

Dr. William Brewster Mather, a medical missionary in Peking (Beijing), was interned in the Philippines with his wife Edith Reed Mather while attending the Chinese Language School in Baguio, which had relocated there from Peking to escape the Japanese occupation of Peking. They were held at the Baguio internment camp, a prewar Philippine Constabulary base also known as Camp Holmes. Their third child, Sarah Anna Mather, was born in the Baguio internment camp. In December 1944 they were moved to Bilibid Prison in Manila, which U.S. forces liberated in February 1945.

Rev. Paul Rutherford Winn, who had been serving in an Episcopalian mission in Soochow (Suzhou), was interned in November 1942 at the Haiphong Road prison camp in Shanghai. (The prison compound, originally built as the mansion of a wealthy Chinese family, had during the 1930s served as a barracks of the 4th Marine Regiment of the U.S. Marine Corps, the "China Marines.") He was exchanged and repatriated to the United States in September 1943 on the MS *Gripsholm*, the same ship used for the repatriation of Americans deported from Korea.

Rev. Gardner Lewis Winn was held at the Santo Tomas prison camp in Manila. The camp, on the campus of the University of Santo Tomas, held more than 4,000 internees from January 1942 until its liberation by U.S. forces in February 1945.

Chapter 7
American Pyongyang Today

Modern Pyongyang, with Kim Il Sung Square next to the river at the left and the pyramid of the unfinished Ryugyong Hotel at the right. The Presbyterian mission once occupied the exact center of this photograph.

Cho Man Sik, the Presbyterian leader of the people's committee in Pyongyang, with Soviet generals at a ceremony commemorating the liberation of Pyongyang from Japanese rule

Rev. Kim Ik Too, a leading Presbyterian pastor who returned from Seoul to the north to minister to Christians left behind north of the 38th Parallel in 1945. North Korean forces killed him after the Inchon landing in September 1950.

The Soviet Army entered Pyongyang on August 24, 1945, beginning the era of Communist rule. Far from finding a populace eager for Communism, they encountered opposition from a people's committee led by Christians, who made up 50,000 of the city's 300,000 people. Its leader was Cho Man Sik, a Presbyterian who had participated in the March First Movement of 1919 and then embraced Mohandas Gandhi's concepts of nonviolent resistance, leading resistance to Japanese rule for a quarter of a century. Soviet troops arrested Cho on January 5, 1946, replacing him and his people's committee with a new body led by Kim Il Sung.

As the North Korean regime became established and repressions against Christians, landowners, and other class enemies grew, Christians and others fled to the south in large numbers. Approximately 750,000 people from the north fled south of the 38th Parallel in 1945-50. Another 650,000 followed during the Korean War in 1950-53. These movements of refugees left behind only a small remnant of Pyongyang's Christians to continue living under North Korean rule.

The regime ruthlessly destroyed remnants of Pyongyang's past during and after the Korean War, killing numerous clergymen and other possible opponents as its forces retreated after the Inchon landing in September 1950. They included Cho Man Sik, reportedly executed with other political prisoners in October 1950. Propaganda re-cast Americans and Christians as villains in Korea's past, starting a destruction of the history of Americans in Pyongyang that has been so thorough that practically no memory of it exists anywhere.

Missionary villain character from the 1951 anti-American story "Jackals"

The North Korean regime completed the eradication of Pyongyang's Christian past by tearing down what was left of it and building monumental new structures to glorify itself. The process began immediately after the war, as the regime rebuilt areas extensively damaged during the war. In 1954, construction of Kim Il Sung Square began and finished by August. Kim Il Sung Square is located only one city block away from the former location of the Presbyterian mission in Pyongyang, at the foot of Namsan Hill, once the site of the residences of the early American missionaries who brought the Presbyterian Church to Pyongyang and educated the first Korean Presbyterian clergy. Namsan Hill is now occupied by the Grand People's Study House, a colossal library built in 1982 that is the main national center for the study of Kim Il Sung and the *Juche* ideology that he created for the North Korean state.

Kim Il Sung Square has become known around the world as the stage for military parades and other mass public spectacles of the North Korean regime. The Grand People's Study House serves as an icon of the regime and its ideology and the backdrop for scenes of all kinds on Kim Il Sung Square. Both have become favorite landmarks where foreign tourists take photographs of themselves. Among the millions of people who have seen Kim Il Sung Square and the Grand People's Study House, few if any have known the history of their location.

Church field day in front of the American mission residences on Namsan Hill. c. 1921

Kim Il Sung Square and the Grand People's Study House on Namsan Hill

West Gate Church, with Union Theological Seminary visible in the background, 1920s

Mansudae Art Theater

Only a block from the northern edge of Kim Il Sung Square, the entrance to the Presbyterian mission is occupied by Mansudae Art Theater, another signature edifice of the North Korean regime. Mansudae Art Theater and its grounds occupy land that once held West Gate Church, Union Theological Seminary, and Union Christian Hospital. Built in 1976, the theater has 60,000 square meters of floor space and serves as the stage for many of the largest indoor official spectacles of the North Korean regime. They have included the welcoming ceremonies for the visit of the New York Philharmonic in 2008.

The theater complex and the adjacent fountains are another location popular with foreign tourists. They are certainly as unaware of what once existed on the site as they are when visiting Kim Il Sung Square and the Grand People's Study House.

Across the street from Mansudae Art Theater, the former campus of Union Christian College is now the site of the Embassy of Russia in Pyongyang. Union Christian College came under Soviet control immediately after the Red Army entered Pyongyang, its modern buildings and large athletic fields making it ideal for use as a military headquarters and a tank park. Once the center of American Christian influence in Pyongyang, the place became the center of Soviet Communist influence in North Korea. The Embassy of Russia now occupies the site, built over the former locations of Union Christian College, Pyongyang Foreign School, and the Sungshil Academy that Kim Il Sung's father attended in the 1900s.

Union Christian College, early 1900s

The Embassy of Russia in Pyongyang

A successor to Union Christian College emerged soon after the Korean War in Seoul, which became the center of Korean Presbyterianism after 1945. A new Sungshil University opened in 1954, continuing the name and history of the original Sungshil Academy and Union Christian College in Pyongyang.

A remnant of American Pyongyang continues to exist in North Korea, where reports of underground believers indicate that Christians have survived in hiding into the 21st Century. They are a legacy of the American Christian presence in Pyongyang from 1895 to 1942, largely forgotten in both the United States and Korea but of ongoing relevance to the problem of North Korea that has imprisoned over 25 million Koreans under the Kim Il Sung regime.

North view of Union Christian College, 1933

North view of the current Pyongyang skyline, with the unfinished Ryugyong Hotel on the left

The End – For Now

Request for Additional Information

The photographs and narrative in this book represent the best that could be done with limited existing primary and secondary literature and the advice and assistance of a very small number of descendants of Americans from the missionary community in Pyongyang. They were only a small fraction of the thousands of descendants of the hundreds who lived there from 1895 to 1942. A more complete account will be possible with the assistance of additional individuals with family memories and mementoes of the era, so the author invites anyone with something to share about American Pyongyang – American or Korean – to contact him. Contact can be made by email to americanpyongyang@gmail.com.

About the Author

Robert Kim is a second generation American with forebears from the Haeju, Seoul and Jindo areas, in both South and North Korea. He is a lawyer by profession and has served for many years in government and in foreign affairs, including a term in Iraq as the Deputy Attaché from the U.S. Department of the Treasury in 2009-10. He was raised, and currently lives, in the Washington, DC area.

Acknowledgments

Reconstructing and explaining the history presented in these pages was possible thanks to the efforts of a few institutions and individuals to preserve evidence and memories of the American Christian presence in Pyongyang that ended 75 years ago.

Three archives provided most of the material for this book. The Presbyterian Historical Society in Philadelphia, Pennsylvania preserves a large collection of records, photographs and other artifacts of the Presbyterian mission in Pyongyang and the Presbyterian Church in Korea that provided the foundation of knowledge and most of the photographs for this book. The Princeton Theological Seminary Library in Princeton, New Jersey preserves a Special Collection donated by Dr. Samuel H. Moffett, son of Pyongyang mission founder Rev. Samuel A. Moffett, and Eileen F. Moffett, with a substantial body of personal papers, photographs and literature about the American presence in Pyongyang. The Burke Library Archives of Union Theological Seminary, Columbia University, provided additional material.

Several individuals provided crucial insights and anecdotes, as well as photographs from their personal collections. The actions and character of the Rev. George S. McCune and his family were made clearer by several of his descendants. Helen McCune Lawless, daughter of George M. McCune and Evelyn Becker McCune and granddaughter of Rev. George S. McCune, shared many memories, photographs and books of her father, mother and grandfather. Antoinette McCune Bement did the same for her father Shannon McCune and grandfather, as did Marilyn Becker Peters for her father Maxwell Becker and grandfather Arthur Becker.

Additional insight into the early Presbyterian mission in Pyongyang and the role of Dr. J. Hunter Wells came from Barbara Wells Howarth, granddaughter of Dr. Wells. Her upcoming biography of her grandfather should be an additional valuable resource for understanding the American Christian presence in Pyongyang.

Notes on Sources

Frontispiece

The map shown is a small excerpt from a U.S. Army Map Service map of Pyongyang, A.M.S. L951, dated 1946. This map clearly was a translation of a Japanese map of the Second World War era, as it includes place names in both Japanese and Korean, Japanese military bases (e.g. "Barracks 77th Infantry Regiment"), and industries with Japanese names ("Nippon Oil Co.," "Japan Corn Products Co.," "Fuji Iron Works" and "Showa Aircraft Plant"). The translator of this map would have been Helen Becker McCune, who during the war worked as a Korean and Japanese translator for the Army Map Service.

Chapter 1

All images in this chapter are from the archives of the Presbyterian Historical Society, with the following exceptions. The photographs of King Gojong (p. 3) and of a Righteous Army (p. 10) are from Wikimedia. The photograph of the Revs. William Swallen, Graham Lee and Samuel Moffett preparing for their journey from Seoul to Pyongyang (p. 5) is from the Special Collection of the papers of Samuel H. Moffett (shown as goaltender of the Pyongyang Foreign School hockey team, p. 49) at the Princeton Theological Seminary Library. The photographs of Dr. J. Hunter Wells and his "cholera corps" in 1902 (p. 8) and of Dr. Wells, Dr. G.M. Wells, and four Korean doctors in 1911 (p. 12) are from the collection of Barbara Wells Howarth.

Chapter 2

All images in this chapter are from the archives of the Presbyterian Historical Society, with the following exceptions.

The map of Union Christian College and the Presbyterian mission (p. 16) is from the collection of Helen McCune Lawless. Her mother, Helen Becker McCune, drew the map by hand on the back of a November 17, 1931 letter from her father in law, Rev. George S. McCune. This unofficial map, which accurately renders the details of buildings down to the shapes of their roofs and the number and layout of their windows, may be the most detailed map of the Presbyterian mission that has survived, and it was essential to figuring out the layout of the mission and the relationship between its buildings and those of modern-day Pyongyang.

The photographs of the Pyongyang Red Cross in 1912 (p. 21) and of Dr. Wells attending a medical school graduation ceremony in 1914 (p. 22) are from the collection of Barbara Wells Howarth.

The photographs of prisoners from the One Hundred Five (p. 27) and of the March First Movement (p. 28) are from the collection of Antoinette McCune Bement, inherited from her father, Dr. Shannon McCune, younger son of the Rev. George S. McCune. Shannon McCune had been closely connected to both events, having received his Korean name Yun An-Paik from political prisoners from the One Hundred Five and witnessed the March First Movement as a six year old child. Shannon McCune was a professor of geography and accumulated a large collection of ancient Korean maps that currently resides in the Library of Congress.

Chapter 3

The 1933 school yearbook of Union Christian College, donated to the archives of the Presbyterian Historical Society by Antoinette McCune Bement, was the source of all of the images in this chapter. The archive also has a 1930 Union Christian College yearbook.

Chapter 4

Pyongyang Foreign School yearbooks ("*Kulsi's*") from various years and a master history published in 1943, which have survived in the archives of the Presbyterian Historical Society, were the sources of the images and information in this chapter. The *Master Kulsi*, published in

1943 by the principal of Pyongyang Foreign School as a summary of all past yearbooks, was the source for the images on pages 43 through 46 and the photo of Boy Scout Troop 1 of Pyongyang on page 52. The image of girls' athletics on page 47 was from the 1933 *Kulsi*. The 1934 basketball team yearbook story on page 48 was from the 1934 *Kulsi*. The images and history of the ice hockey team on pages 49 through 51 were from the 1933, 1934 and 1936 *Kulsi*'s. The party stories and *Merchant of Venice* collage on pages 53 through 55 were from the 1933 *Kulsi*. The school song on page 56 is from the 1936 *Kulsi*.

Chapter 5

The 1938 and 1941 mission group photographs on pages 57 and 59 are from the archives of the Presbyterian Historical Society. The 1940 Pyongyang Foreign School photograph on page 58 is from the *Master Kulsi*. The newspaper clipping of the MS *Gripsholm* on page 60 is from the *Shanghai Evening Post American Edition,* Dec. 3, 1943, in the Foreign Missions Conference of North America Records, The Burke Library Archives, Union Theological Seminary, Columbia University.

Chapter 6

The photographs of George M. McCune and Evelyn Becker McCune on pages 61 and 62 are from the collection of Helen McCune Lawless. The photographs of Maxwell Becker on pages 63 and 64 are from the collection of Marilyn Peters. The photographs of Shannon McCune on page 65 are from the collection of Antoinette McCune Bement.

All information on alumni and other former students of Pyongyang Foreign School in the Second World War on pages 66 through 74 are from the *Master Kulsi*.

Chapter 7

The photographs of Rev. Kim Ik Too, the American mission residences, West Gate Church, and Union Christian College on pages 76 through 81 are from the archives of the Presbyterian Historical Society. All color photographs in this chapter are public domain images from Wikimedia.

Made in the USA
Middletown, DE
18 April 2017